Striding Slippers

ADAPTED FROM AN UDMURT TALE BY

Mirra Ginsburg

PICTURES BY

Sal Murdocca

MACMILLAN PUBLISHING CO., INC.

New York

COLLIER MACMILLAN PUBLISHERS

London

Macmillan Publishing Co., Inc.
866 Third Avenue, New York, N.Y. 10022
Collier Macmillan Canada, Ltd.
Printed in the United States of America
10 9 8 7 6 5 4 3 2 1

Library of Congress Cataloging in Publication Data

Ginsburg, Mirra. Striding slippers.
Summary: Magical striding slippers are stolen from the shepherd who made them, but they cannot be controlled by anyone else.
[1. Folklore—Udmurt A.S.S.R. 2. Folklore—Russia]
I. Murdocca, Sal. II. Title.
PZ8.1.G455Ss [398.2] [E] 77-12035
ISBN 0-02-736370-8

To Phyllis and Alan

Once there lived a shepherd. He had many cows and sheep to look after, and as his herd increased, his work became more and more difficult. The cows would wander off into the cornfields, the sheep would get bogged down in the swamps, the calves would scatter through the woods. The shepherd had his hands full, searching for the animals, driving them back to the meadow, and trying to keep them all together where they would be safe and out of mischief. Day after day the poor shepherd would tire himself out till he could barely walk.

Then he said to himself:

"I'll make myself a pair of striding slippers. They'll carry me and I won't get so tired."

He peeled strips of bark from some linden trees and sat down to work. He worked and worked, and wove himself a pair of fine bast slippers—not ordinary ones, but fast-striding ones. A single step, and he would be across the field. Another, and the field was far behind. Now it became much easier for him to tend his herd.

One hot day the shepherd sat down on a hillock to have his lunch. He took off his striding slippers and put them down on the ground nearby. Just then a passing stranger greeted him and sat down beside him.

"How do you manage to look after such a large herd?" he asked.

"Ah," laughed the shepherd. "I have striding slippers. Every step takes me a mile."

"Where did you find such slippers?" asked the stranger.

"I didn't find them, I made them myself," the shepherd answered. "I walked through the woods for seven days, peeling off just the right kind of bark. Then I stayed up for seven nights to weave the slippers. Nobody can weave as I do. These slippers will never wear out, and they will carry me across wide rivers and dense forests, wherever I wish to go."

The stranger listened to the shepherd and thought to himself:

"I'm still a long way from my cousin's village. My own slippers are worn to shreds. His are fresh and new, and they are striding ones! I'll steal them."

He waited till the shepherd turned away, then he threw off his torn slippers and quickly stepped into the shepherd's. The striding slippers creaked and carried him away, fast as the wind. They carried him across the field, along the road.

Before he knew it, he had passed the village where his cousin lived, and had to turn back. The village came in sight again, and then his cousin's house. But he could not stop. The striding slippers carried him on and on.

He turned once more and tried to direct his steps toward his cousin's gate, but the slippers ran so fast that he bumped right into the gatepost. He tumbled on his back. But even there his feet kept striding and striding in the air.

The village children gathered around him and stared in wonder.

The peasant cried:

"Help me! Take the slippers off my feet! I'll give you cakes and candy."

The children came closer and tried to catch his feet. But the feet kept running and running in the air, and the children could not get hold of them.

"All together now! Try again!"

Well, they tried and tried, and finally they managed to pull off the slippers. The peasant caught his breath, got up, and said:

"Seven times seven curses on those striding slippers! A man must know how to use them. It serves me right. I'm lucky you got them off, or else who knows where they would have taken me."

“Where did you get such slippers, uncle?” the children asked.

But the peasant was ashamed to tell them the truth.

“Oh, out that way,” he mumbled. “From a shepherd . . . I took them, and now I’m afraid of them myself.”

He gave the children cakes and candy. Then he slung the striding slippers over his shoulder and walked into his cousin’s house with bare feet.

At his cousin’s house there was a celebration. The guests were dressed up in their finest. They sat around the table, drinking, eating, singing songs.

The cousin welcomed him, but then glanced down at his bare feet and asked:

“Why do you come here barefoot?”

What could the man say? He was ashamed to tell the truth, and so he lied:

"My slippers are a bit too small. They hurt my feet."

He sat down, put the slippers under the bench, and began to eat and drink and sing like everybody else.

Next to him sat another guest, with a red beard. He glanced at the slippers and thought:

"Just right for me."

Quietly he threw off his old slippers and put on the new ones. They were neither too big nor too small—exactly his size. He stood up, took a step, and flew out of the house as if caught up by a storm wind.

Before the other guests could gasp or blink an eye, the redbeard was gone. He clattered down the steps and banged against the hitching post. The striding slippers carried him off and away—through the gate and down the street in a swirling cloud of dust. Frightened hens flew up on fences, geese scrambled into the pond, children scattered in all directions.

"Help! Stop me!" he yelled with all his might.

But the slippers carried him on and on, across the field and toward the woods. Luckily, he bumped into a fence, caught hold of a fence post, and tumbled on his back. And his feet kept striding and striding in the air. The other guests came running and managed after a while to remove the slippers. For a long time the redbeard could not say a word. Then he began to mutter, over and over again:

"Oh, my, it serves me right.... It serves me right!"

At this moment a merchant happened to be driving past. He saw the crowd and stopped to ask:

"What's all the excitement about? What happened? Why is everybody staring at those slippers? What's so marvelous about them?"

"They're marvelous, all right," the peasants answered. "They aren't ordinary slippers—they're striding ones. This fellow put them on, and in a minute he was across the field."

The merchant's eyes lit up with greed.

"Whose slippers are they?" he asked. "Who owns them? I'll buy them!"

But no one would admit to owning the slippers. So the merchant said:

"If there's no owner, I will take them."

He took them and drove on.

This merchant, now, was a hard and cruel man. He starved his workman, never gave him a moment's rest, and made him do the work of ten. All that the poor man heard from him was "Faster!" "Slowpoke!" "Hurry up!"

And the merchant thought to himself as he drove away:

"With these marvelous slippers my workman will do the work of twenty men."

As soon as he drove into the yard, he shouted to the workman:

"Hey, slowpoke! Hurry up, put on these striding slippers! And get to work. Prepare feed for the horses, then bring water, then go into the woods and get some firewood, then gather all the cabbages in the garden. You understand?"

"I guess I do," the workman said. "It's clear enough."

He put on the slippers. But before he had time to lift a foot they carried him across the yard, into the barn, and plunked him right into the flour bin. He struggled in the bin. His feet kept striding and striding, and the flour rose like a huge white cloud. The merchant came running and began to scold:

"You good-for-nothing, what are you doing? Stop scattering my flour all over the yard!"

But the workman could only moan:

"Oh, pull me out of here! Oh, grab my feet! Oh, I'm choking!"

The merchant threw himself upon the man, dragged him out of the bin, pulled off the striding slippers, and began to thrash him.

"You lazy fool!" he cried. "If you don't work, I will not feed you! Don't you know how to walk in striding slippers?"

"I guess I don't," replied the workman.

"You don't!" the merchant shouted. "Then I will show you! Just watch, I'll put them on myself."

The merchant put on the slippers, took one step, and flew out of the barn like a bullet out of a gun. He tried to catch hold of a horse cart, but he missed it and rushed on. He banged himself against the stable wall, turned a somersault, and tumbled into a trough with swill for the pigs.

Then he flew outside the gate, through puddles, ditches, over fields and rivers, on and on, until he reached the woods and tripped over a stump. There he lay, flat on his back, his feet striding and striding in the air, and shouted with what little breath he still had in his lungs:

"Help! Save me, somebody! Get these devil's slippers off my feet! Oh, oh, they'll be the death of me!"

The shepherd heard him and came running to see what happened. He looked down at the merchant and asked:

"Where did you get my slippers?"

But by now the merchant had lost his voice and could not say a word. The shepherd took his slippers off the merchant's feet and drove him out of the field with his stick, like a straying cow. The greedy merchant staggered back toward the village, disheveled, dirty, his clothes in rags, his face and body full of bumps and bruises.

The shepherd looked over the striding slippers to make sure they were not damaged, put them on, and calmly went back to tending his large herd.

And everybody said he was the best shepherd in the land. He never lost a single cow or calf or sheep, no matter how far they strayed, and never in his life felt tired again.